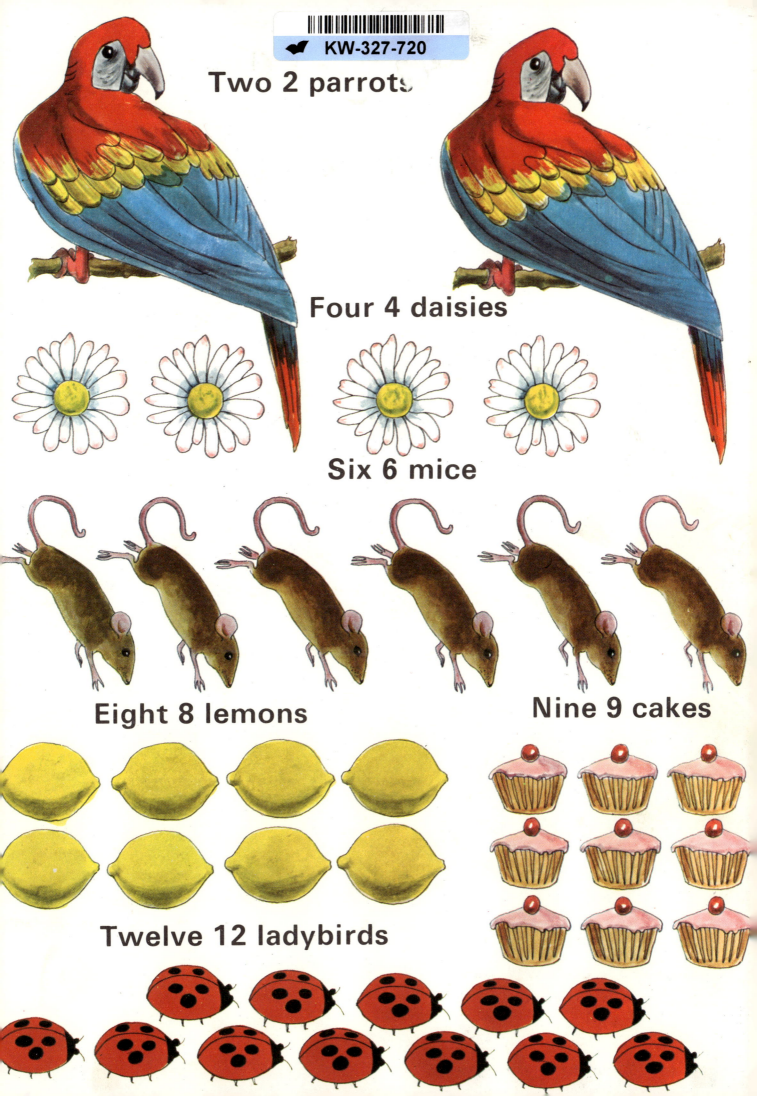

Two 2 parrots

Four 4 daisies

Six 6 mice

Eight 8 lemons

Nine 9 cakes

Twelve 12 ladybirds

Prepared in consultation with Mary M. Turnor,
Head Teacher of Colchester Monkwick Junior School.

Published by Purnell
© 1971 by Purnell and Sons Limited, London
Reprinted in 1972
Made and printed in Great Britain by
Purnell and Sons Ltd., Paulton (Somerset) and London
SBN 361 01818 5

Purnell's PICTURE DICTIONARY in colour

By Moira Maclean

Illustrated by Colin and Moira Maclean and Adrian Purkis

PURNELL
London

Aa

about

The wind blows the
leaves about.
It blows them here and there.
Tell me a story about the wind.
Is it near tea-time?
Is it about tea-time?

above

Put your hand above your head.
It will be higher than your head.

absent

Peter was absent from school.
He was not there.

accident

The driver drove the bus
into the wall.
It was an accident.
He did not mean to drive
into the wall.

ache

Peter has an ache in his tooth.
He has a pain in his tooth.
He has toothache.

across

John walks across the road.
He is going to the other side.

act

Actors act in plays.
They play a part.
They are acting.

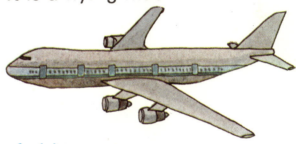

add

If you add one and one
together you have two.
You put them together.

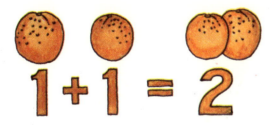

address

Your address tells us
where you live.
You write an address
on a letter.

Miss Jane Smith,
46, Willow Drive,
Yorkhampton,
Glos.   12H 2B

admire

We admire brave people.
We like to know about them.

aeroplane

An aeroplane flies in the sky.
It is a flying machine.

afraid

You should not be afraid
of a spider.
You should not fear it.

after

Mark ran after his sister.
He ran behind her.

Aa
Bb
Cc
Dd
Ee
Ff
Gg
Hh
Ii
Jj
Kk
Ll
Mm
Nn
Oo
Pp
Qq
Rr
Ss
Tt
Uu
Vv
Ww
Xx
Yy
Zz

again
You can write your name again.
You can do it more than once.

against
Jill leans against the wall.

age
What is your age?
How old are you?

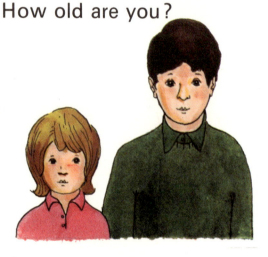

air
We all breathe air.
Birds fly in the air.

alive
You are alive.
You are living.

all
All the boys play football.
Every boy is playing.

almost
Simon almost fell off
the swing.
He nearly fell off it.

alone
Mary is alone.
There is no one with her.

along
Peter is walking
along the road.

alphabet
The **alphabet** is all
the letters we use.
There are twenty-six letters
in our **alphabet**.

also
The dog has four legs
It **also** has a tail.

always
Always try to be good.
Try to be good at all times.

angry
Jill is **angry**.
Someone has spilled her drink.
She is not pleased.

animal
A giraffe is an **animal**.
It is a live creature that
can move and feel.

ankle
Your **ankle** is the joint
above your foot.
It helps you to move your foot.

Aa
Bb
Cc
Dd
Ee
Ff
Gg
Hh
Ii
Jj
Kk
Ll
Mm
Nn
Oo
Pp
Qq
Rr
Ss
Tt
Uu
Vv
Ww
Xx
Yy
Zz

Aa
Bb
Cc
Dd
Ee
Ff
Gg
Hh
Ii
Jj
Kk
Ll
Mm
Nn
Oo
Pp
Qq
Rr
Ss
Tt
Uu
Vv
Ww
Xx
Yy
Zz

another
Susan needs another shoe.
She needs one more shoe.

answer
Ask a question.
Someone will answer it.

any
Peter may choose any apple
from the tree.
He may choose whichever
one he likes.

anything
Do you know anything
about birds?
Do you know one thing
about them?

ape
An ape is a wild animal.
You can see an ape at the zoo.

apple
An apple is a fruit.
It is good to eat.
Apples grow on trees.

April
April is the name of a month.
It is the fourth month
of the year.

arm
You have two arms.
You have a right arm and
a left arm.

army

A very large number of soldiers is called an army.

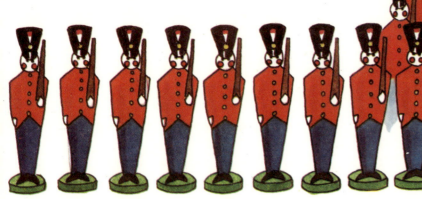

arrive

The train will arrive at the station.
We will wait for it to come.

arrow

An arrow is a stick with a sharp point at one end.

artist

An artist paints pictures.

as

Peter is as tall as Mark.

ask

You ask a question.
You ask for what you want.

asleep

The cat is asleep.
It is not awake.

Aa
Bb
Cc
Dd
Ee
Ff
Gg
Hh
Ii
Jj
Kk
Ll
Mm
Nn
Oo
Pp
Qq
Rr
Ss
Tt
Uu
Vv
Ww
Xx
Yy
Zz

Aa
Bb
Cc
Dd
Ee
Ff
Gg
Hh
Ii
Jj
Kk
Ll
Mm
Nn
Oo
Pp
Qq
Rr
Ss
Tt
Uu
Vv
Ww
Xx
Yy
Zz

at
You are at home.
That is where you are.

ate
Peter ate all his dinner.
When he had eaten it
there was none left.

August
August is the name of a month.
It is in summer.

aunt
Your aunt is your mother's or
your father's sister.

Autumn
Autumn is one of the seasons
of the year.
The leaves fall from the
trees in autumn.

awake
The rabbit is awake.
It is not asleep.

away
The sailor sailed away
in his ship.
He was not at home.
He was away.

Bb

baby
A baby is a young child.

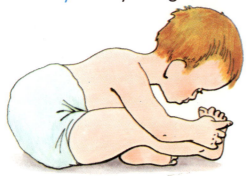

bake
We bake bread and cakes
in an oven.

bank
We put money in a bank
to keep it safe.
This is a piggy-bank.
Another kind of bank
is the side of a river.

bark
Dogs bark.
A tree has a covering skin
of bark.

barn
The farmer keeps his hay
in a barn.

bat
Mark hits the ball with a bat.
Another kind of bat flies
in the air at night.

Aa
Bb
Cc
Dd
Ee
Ff
Gg
Hh
Ii
Jj
Kk
Ll
Mm
Nn
Oo
Pp
Qq
Rr
Ss
Tt
Uu
Vv
Ww
Xx
Yy
Zz

Aa
Bb
Cc
Dd
Ee
Ff
Gg
Hh
Ii
Jj
Kk
Ll
Mm
Nn
Oo
Pp
Qq
Rr
Ss
Tt
Uu
Vv
Ww
Xx
Yy
Zz

bath
We wash in a bath.
Then we are clean all over.

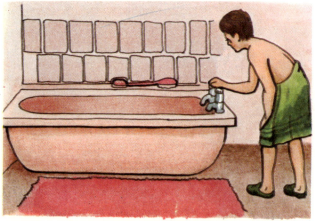

battery
Your torch will shine if it has a battery in it.

beach
The beach at the seaside is nice and sandy.

beak
A bird has a beak.
It pecks with its beak.

bear
A bear is a wild animal.

bee
A bee is an insect.
It makes honey.

beetle
A beetle is an insect.

behind

Peter is hiding behind
the tree.
The tree is in front of Peter.

believe

When you believe a story,
you think it is true.

belong

Does this book belong to you?
Is it your book?

below

The red book is below
the green book.
It is under the green book.

bend

When you bend your arm,
it is not straight.

berry

A berry is a small fruit.

beside

Mother sits beside Father.
She sits by the side of Father.

Aa
Bb
Cc
Dd
Ee
Ff
Gg
Hh
Ii
Jj
Kk
Ll
Mm
Nn
Oo
Pp
Qq
Rr
Ss
Tt
Uu
Vv
Ww
Xx
Yy
Zz

Aa
Bb
Cc
Dd
Ee
Ff
Gg
Hh
Ii
Jj
Kk
Ll
Mm
Nn
Oo
Pp
Qq
Rr
Ss
Tt
Uu
Vv
Ww
Xx
Yy
Zz

between

The red box is between the two blue boxes.

bicycle

A bicycle has two wheels, one behind the other.

bird

A bird has wings and feathers. It can fly from place to place.

birthday

You have a birthday every year. Your birthday is the date on which you were born.

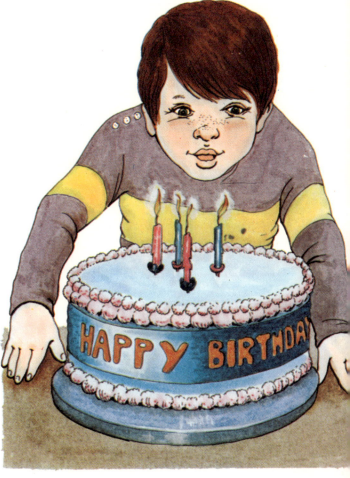

blood

Blood is a red liquid.

boat

A boat sails on the water.

boil
Mother must boil water
to make tea.

bonfire
A bonfire is a fire in the garden.

book
A book is a number of sheets
of paper fastened together.

boot
You wear boots on your feet.
Another kind of boot is a place
for luggage in a car.

bottle
A bottle holds things.
Most bottles are made of glass.

bowl
The Three Bears each had a
bowl of porridge.

branch
Mark can swing on a branch
of the tree.

brick
A brick is used for building.

Aa
Bb
Cc
Dd
Ee
Ff
Gg
Hh
Ii
Jj
Kk
Ll
Mm
Nn
Oo
Pp
Qq
Rr
Ss
Tt
Uu
Vv
Ww
Xx
Yy
Zz

17

Aa
Bb
Cc
Dd
Ee
Ff
Gg
Hh
Ii
Jj
Kk
Ll
Mm
Nn
Oo
Pp
Qq
Rr
Ss
Tt
Uu
Vv
Ww
Xx
Yy
Zz

bridge
A bridge goes over a river or a road or a railway.

brother
A boy is the brother of the other children in the family. They have the same mother and father.

brush
Mother sweeps with a brush.

bubble
A bubble is soap with air inside it.

bucket
Water is carried in a bucket.

budgerigar
A budgerigar is a small bird. This budgerigar is in a cage.

building
A building has walls and a roof.
A house is a building.

bus

A bus is like a big motor car.
It has many seats inside.

bush

A bush looks like a small tree.

busy

When we are busy, we are
working hard.

butterfly

A butterfly is an insect.

button

A button helps us to
fasten our clothes.

buy

Peter is going to the shop to
buy some sweets.

Aa
Bb
Cc
Dd
Ee
Ff
Gg
Hh
Ii
Jj
Kk
Ll Mm
Nn
Oo
Pp
Qq
Rr
Ss
Tt
Uu
Vv
Ww
Xx
Yy
Zz

Aa
Bb
Cc
Dd
Ee
Ff
Gg
Hh
Ii
Jj
Kk
Ll
Mm
Nn
Oo
Pp
Qq
Rr
Ss
Tt
Uu
Vv
Ww
Xx
Yy
Zz

Cc

cabbage

A cabbage is a vegetable.
It has green leaves.
We eat cabbage.

cake

Mother mixes flour, sugar,
and eggs to make a cake.
She bakes the cake in the oven.
We eat cake for tea.

calendar

On a calendar you can count the
days, weeks and months
of the year.

calf

A calf is a young cow or bull.

camel

Look at this animal.
It is a camel.
It lives in the desert.
It has one or two humps
on its back.

camera

Simon is taking a photograph with his camera.

candle

A candle gives a small, yellow light.
We often light candles at Christmas time.

car

We can ride in a motor car.
It has wheels and an engine.

caravan

Have you ever spent a holiday in a caravan?
It is like a house on wheels.

carrot

A carrot is a vegetable.
It grows in the garden.
Mother cooks carrots for dinner.

carry

Ann has a heavy bag to carry.

castle

This big building is a castle.
It was built a long time ago.

Aa
Bb
Cc
Dd
Ee
Ff
Gg
Hh
Ii
Jj
Kk
Ll
Mm
Nn
Oo
Pp
Qq
Rr
Ss
Tt
Uu
Vv
Ww
Xx
Yy
Zz

Aa
Bb
Cc
Dd
Ee
Ff
Gg
Hh
Ii
Jj
Kk
Ll
Mm
Nn
Oo
Pp
Qq
Rr
Ss
Tt
Uu
Vv
Ww
Xx
Yy
Zz

caterpillar
A caterpillar turns into
a butterfly.

cave
A cave is a hole in the ground.

centre
The spot is in the centre of
the square.
It is in the middle of it.

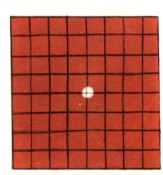

cheap
Anything that does not cost
very much is cheap.

cherry
A cherry is a fruit.
It grows on a tree.
Cherries are good to eat.

chew
You should chew your food well
before you swallow it.

chicken
A chicken is a young bird.
When the chicken grows up
it will be a cock or a hen.

chimney
Look at the tall chimney.
It lets out smoke.

choir

The children sing together.
They are a choir.

Christmas

Christmas is the birthday of Jesus.
Christmas Day is the 25th of December.

circus

There are animals at the circus.
There are funny clowns.
The circus is inside a big tent.

city

A city is a big town.
It has lots of shops and offices and houses.
London is a city.

class

When you are in a class, you are with people who are the same as you.
At school you are in a class.
The children in the class are the same age as you.

claw

A cat's claw is sharp.
Cats scratch with their claws.

Aa
Bb
Cc
Dd
Ee
Ff
Gg
Hh
Ii
Jj
Kk
Ll
Mm
Nn
Oo
Pp
Qq
Rr
Ss
Tt
Uu
Vv
Ww
Xx
Yy
Zz

Aa
Bb
Cc
Dd
Ee
Ff
Gg
Hh
Ii
Jj
Kk
Ll
Mm
Nn
Oo
Pp
Qq
Rr
Ss
Tt
Uu
Vv
Ww
Xx
Yy
Zz

climb

Jane can climb well.
She has climbed the tree.

clock

A clock measures the time.
Can you tell the time on
this clock?

clothes

John hangs up his clothes
before he goes to bed.

cloud

An aeroplane can fly
through a cloud.
In good weather clouds are
white.
A black cloud brings rain.

clumsy

Tim has knocked over the glass
He is clumsy.

collect

Peter likes to collect stamps.
He keeps them all together.

colour

Everything has a colour.
This flower is blue.
That is its colour.
What colour is the leaf?

comic
Anything comic makes us laugh.
A paper with funny stories
and drawings in it
is called a comic.

corner
Where two walls join they
make a corner.
The chair is in the corner.

cost
Jane bought an orange.
It cost three pence.
That is what she paid for it.

cottage
A cottage is a little house
in the country.

cough
When you have a cold
it makes you cough.
A cough is nasty.
It hurts your throat.

count
How many pencils are there?
Can you count them?

country
There are fields and trees
in the country.
A country also means a land.
England is a country.

cousin
Your cousin is the child
of your aunt and uncle.
Your mother and father are
your cousin's aunt and uncle.

cow
A cow is a farm animal.
Our milk comes from a cow.

Aa
Bb
Cc
Dd
Ee
Ff
Gg
Hh
Ii
Jj
Kk
Ll
Mm
Nn
Oo
Pp
Qq
Rr
Ss
Tt
Uu
Vv
Ww
Xx
Yy
Zz

Aa
Bb
Cc
Dd
Ee
Ff
Gg
Hh
Ii
Jj
Kk
Ll
Mm
Nn
Oo
Pp
Qq
Rr
Ss
Tt
Uu
Vv
Ww
Xx
Yy
Zz

cowboy
In America there are big farms with many cows and bulls.
A cowboy looks after them.

crawl
The baby is not able to walk, but she can crawl.

crayon
A crayon is a soft pencil or a stick of colour.

creature
A creature is a living thing.

cricket
Cricket is a game.
A cricket is also an insect.

crocodile
A crocodile is an animal that lives in rivers.
Its skin is tough and hard.

crocus
One of the first flowers in spring is the crocus.

crow
A crow is a big black bird.
A cock makes a noise
called a crow.

crowd
A great many people all
together are called a crowd.

crown
The top of your head is called
the crown.
There is another kind of crown.
It is worn by kings and queens.

crumb
A crumb is a tiny piece.
The mouse eats a bread-crumb.

cuckoo
A cuckoo is a bird.
It calls "cuckoo!".

cupboard
Sarah keeps her room tidy.
She puts her toys in
the cupboard.

curl
When something has a curl it
is bent round.
Jill's hair curls.
John likes to curl up
and read a book.

curtain
The window has a blue curtain.

cut
Anything with a sharp edge
will cut.
Scissors cut paper.

Aa
Bb
Cc
Dd
Ee
Ff
Gg
Hh
Ii
Jj
Kk
Ll
Mm
Nn
Oo
Pp
Qq
Rr
Ss
Tt
Uu
Vv
Ww
Xx
Yy
Zz

Aa
Bb
Cc
Dd
Ee
Ff
Gg
Hh
Ii
Jj
Kk
Ll
Mm
Nn
Oo
Pp
Qq
Rr
Ss
Tt
Uu
Vv
Ww
Xx
Yy
Zz

Dd

daffodil

A daffodil is a spring flower.
It is yellow.

dairy

Milk is made into butter and
cheese in a dairy.
A dairy shop sells milk,
butter and cheese.

daisy

A daisy is a flower with a
yellow centre and white petals.

dance

When we dance we move about
in time to music.

dandelion

A dandelion is a yellow flower.
Its seeds are feathery to
help them float in the air.

danger

Anything that might harm you
is a danger.
If you go too near the
fire you will be in danger.

dare

Peter is brave.
He will dare to jump
into the water.

dark

When there is no light,
it is dark,
It is dark at night.

date

A date is the name and
number of any day.
Friday, May the 6th, is a date.
A date is also a sticky fruit.

daughter

A girl is the daughter of
her father and mother.

December

December is the twelfth month.
It is the last one of the year.

deep

Anything that goes far down
is deep.
Out at sea, the water is deep.

Aa
Bb
Cc
Dd
Ee
Ff
Gg
Hh
Ii
Jj
Kk
Ll
Mm
Nn
Oo
Pp
Qq
Rr
Ss
Tt
Uu
Vv
Ww
Xx
Yy
Zz

Aa
Bb
Cc
Dd
Ee
Ff
Gg
Hh
Ii
Jj
Kk
Ll
Mm
Nn
Oo
Pp
Qq
Rr
Ss
Tt
Uu
Vv
Ww
Xx
Yy
Zz

deer
A deer is an animal
that lives in the woods.

deliver
The postman will deliver
the letters.
He will take them where they
ought to go.

dentist
A dentist cares for our teeth.

desert
Land that is bare and dry
is a desert.
If we go away from a place,
we desert it.

desk
A desk is a table.
We read or write at a desk.

destroy
To destroy something is to
break it or spoil it.

diamond
A diamond is a hard,
sparkly stone.

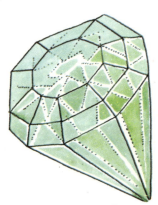

dictionary

This book is a dictionary.
It tells the meaning of
lots of words.

different

The bottles are not the same.
They are different.

difficult

Building a fort is hard to do.
It is difficult.

disappear

The aeroplane will fly into the
cloud and disappear.
We will not be able to see it.

discover

If we find something that
was hidden, we discover it.

distance

Distance is the space between
one place and another.
How far is it from your house
to the bus-stop?
What is the distance?

Aa
Bb
Cc
Dd
Ee
Ff
Gg
Hh
Ii
Jj
Kk
Ll
Mm
Nn
Oo
Pp
Qq
Rr
Ss
Tt
Uu
Vv
Ww
Xx
Yy
Zz

Aa
Bb
Cc
Dd
Ee
Ff
Gg
Hh
Ii
Jj
Kk
Ll
Mm
Nn
Oo
Pp
Qq
Rr
Ss
Tt
Uu
Vv
Ww
Xx
Yy
Zz

dive

To dive is to go into water head first.
Simon is diving into the pool.

divide

When we divide something, we make it into smaller pieces.

doctor

A doctor looks after your health.
If you are ill, the doctor helps you to get well again.

donkey

A donkey is an animal with long ears.

double

To double something is to add the same again.
If you have two lemons, and you add another two, you have doubled your lemons.

down

When you go down, you go to a lower place.
John is going down the stairs.

dozen

A dozen means twelve.
Here are a dozen cakes.

dragon

A dragon is a fierce animal.
It is not real.
Dragons only happen in stories.

draw

You can draw a picture.
To draw something also means
to pull it.

dream

When we are asleep we dream.
A dream is like a story.

drink

When we drink we
swallow liquid.
Jill will drink her milk.

drive

The milkman can drive his van.
He can make it go wherever
he wants it to go.

drop

A drop is something that falls.
A raindrop falls from the sky.
If you drop something,
you let it fall.

drum

A drum is hollow inside.
The baby beats his drum.
It makes a loud noise.

dry

When something is dry,
it is not wet.
Mother hangs the washing up
to let it dry.

duck

A duck is a bird that can swim,
and can duck under the water.

Aa
Bb
Cc
Dd
Ee
Ff
Gg
Hh
Ii
Jj
Kk
Ll
Mm
Nn
Oo
Pp
Qq
Rr
Ss
Tt
Uu
Vv
Ww
Xx
Yy
Zz

D.—C

Aa
Bb
Cc
Dd
Ee
Ff
Gg
Hh
Ii
Jj
Kk
Ll
Mm
Nn
Oo
Pp
Qq
Rr
Ss
Tt
Uu
Vv
Ww
Xx
Yy
Zz

Ee

each

There is an apple on each plate, and each one has a leaf.

eagle

An eagle is a large bird. Eagles live high up in the mountains.

ear

You have a right ear and a left ear.
There is one on each side of your head.
You hear with your ears.

early

Ann is early for breakfast. It is not ready yet.

earn

Father will pay Mark for digging the garden. Mark will earn the money.

earth

Plants grow in the earth. Our world is called the earth.

Easter

Church bells ring at Easter. We all have Easter eggs.

easy
It is not hard to catch a ball.
It is easy.

egg
A bird lays an egg.
The baby bird will come
out of the egg.

either
Either Tim or John will
win the race.
One or the other will win it.

elbow
Your elbow is a joint
in your arm.
It helps you to bend your arm.

electric
Most lights are electric.
They work by electricity.

elephant
An elephant is an animal.
It is the biggest four-legged
animal in the world.

empty
There is nothing in the glass.
It is empty.

end
The end is the last part.
The gate is at the end
of the lane.

Aa
Bb
Cc
Dd
Ee
Ff
Gg
Hh
Ii
Jj
Kk
Ll
Mm
Nn
Oo
Pp
Qq
Rr
Ss
Tt
Uu
Vv
Ww
Xx
Yy
Zz

Aa
Bb
Cc
Dd
Ee
Ff
Gg
Hh
Ii
Jj
Kk
Ll
Mm
Nn
Oo
Pp
Qq
Rr
Ss
Tt
Uu
Vv
Ww
Xx
Yy
Zz

engine

An engine is a machine with
a number of parts.
It often pulls or pushes
things to make them go.

enjoy

Did you enjoy the picnic?
Did you feel happy?

enough

There is enough water to
fill the glass.
There is as much as is needed.

entrance

An entrance is a way in.
The door is the entrance
to the house.

envy

Jane has a new puppy.
Her friends envy her.
They would like to have
a puppy too.

equal

The bricks are equal in size.
They are the same size.
The piles of bricks are equal
in number.
There are the same number
of bricks in each pile.

errand

Tim's mother has sent him
to post a letter.
She has sent him on an errand.

escape

To escape is to get out
or get away from.
The lion's cage has strong bars.
The lion must not escape.

even

When something is flat
and smooth, it is even.
Things that are equal are even.

every

Mary has fed all the chickens.
She has fed every chicken.

excite

The fair will excite Peter.
It will thrill him to ride
on the roundabout.

excuse

Ann has been away from school.
She has a good excuse.
She has been ill.
The teacher will not blame Ann.
She will excuse her.

exit

An exit is a way out.

expect

John did not expect it to snow.
He was surprised when it
started to snow.

eye

We have a right eye
and a left eye.
We see with our eyes.

Aa
Bb
Cc
Dd
Ee
Ff
Gg
Hh
Ii
Jj
Kk
Ll
Mm
Nn
Oo
Pp
Qq
Rr
Ss
Tt
Uu
Vv
Ww
Xx
Yy
Zz

Aa
Bb
Cc
Dd
Ee
Ff
Gg
Hh
Ii
Jj
Kk
Ll
Mm
Nn
Oo
Pp
Qq
Rr
Ss
Tt
Uu
Vv
Ww
Xx
Yy
Zz

Ff

face

Your face is the front part
of your head.
Your eyes, nose and mouth
are parts of your face.

fact

Anything that is true
is a fact.

factory

A factory is a building
where people work.
All kinds of things can be
made in a factory.

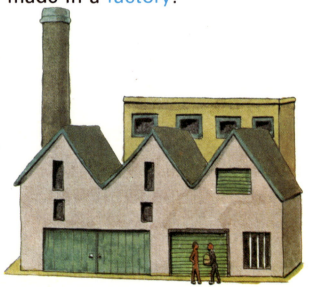

fair

A fair is full of roundabouts
and other things to enjoy.
Fair also means good.
Fair weather is good weather.
Hair that is fair is
a light colour.

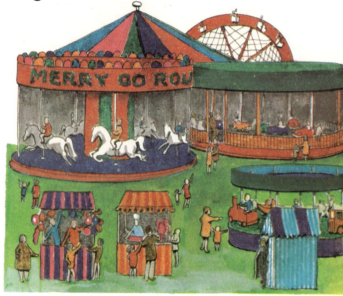

fall

To fall is to drop down.
The leaves fall from the trees.

family

A family means parents
and their children
and uncles, aunts and cousins.

far
Anything that is far
is not near.
The stars are too far
for us to reach.

farm
Much of our food
comes from a farm.
The farmer grows wheat
and oats for our bread.
He keeps cows and hens
to give us milk and eggs.

fast
Anything that is fast
is not slow.
Jill won the race.
She can run very fast.

fat
The farmer is fat.
His wife is thin.

feather
This is a feather.
Feathers grow on birds.

February
February is the second
month of the year.
It is often cold.

Aa
Bb
Cc
Dd
Ee
Ff
Gg
Hh
Ii
Jj
Kk
Ll
Mm
Nn
Oo
Pp
Qq
Rr
Ss
Tt
Uu
Vv
Ww
Xx
Yy
Zz

Aa
Bb
Cc
Dd
Ee
Ff
Gg
Hh
Ii
Jj
Kk
Ll
Mm
Nn
Oo
Pp
Qq
Rr
Ss
Tt
Uu
Vv
Ww
Xx
Yy
Zz

few
Few means not many.
There are few leaves
on the tree.

fierce
The rhinoceros might harm you.
It is fierce

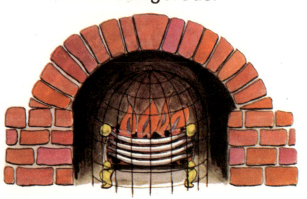

finger
You have a nail on each
finger of your hand.

finish
When will you finish your book?
When will you come
to the end of it?

fire
A fire burns.
It is bright and it warms us.
Fire can be dangerous.

fire-engine
A fire-engine takes firemen
to big fires.
It carries hoses
and ladders to help them
put out the fires.

fireworks
Fireworks make bright lights
and loud bangs.
You should not go
too close to fireworks.

first
The first month of the year
is January.
It is before all the others.

fish

A fish lives in the water.
It has fins and a tail
to help it to swim.

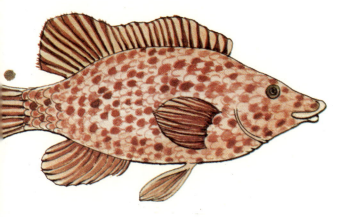

fix

To fix something is to
stick it firmly on,
or to put it right.

flag

A flag is a piece of cloth
that is fixed on to a stick.
Each country has its own flag.

flat

The top of a table is flat.
It is straight and even.
A set of rooms on
one floor of a building
is called a flat.

float

The toy duck will float
on the water.
It will not sink.

flour

Flour is made from grain.
We make bread
and cakes with flour.

Aa
Bb
Cc
Dd
Ee
Ff
Gg
Hh
Ii
Jj
Kk
Ll
Mm
Nn
Oo
Pp
Qq
Rr
Ss
Tt
Uu
Vv
Ww
Xx
Yy
Zz

Aa
Bb
Cc
Dd
Ee
Ff
Gg
Hh
Ii
Jj
Kk
Ll
Mm
Nn
Oo
Pp
Qq
Rr
Ss
Tt
Uu
Vv
Ww
Xx
Yy
Zz

flower
A rose is a flower.

fly
Birds can fly.
A fly is an insect that flies.

foal
A foal is a baby horse.

fog
It is hard to see through a fog.

follow
Susan will follow Mary.
She will go after her.

food
Food is what we eat.

foot
We have five toes on each foot.
The foot of something is the lowest part of it.

forehead
Your forehead is the part of your face above your eyes.

forest

A forest is a large number of trees all growing together.

forget

If you forget something you do not remember it.

forgive

Mark will forgive John for bumping into him. He will not be angry.

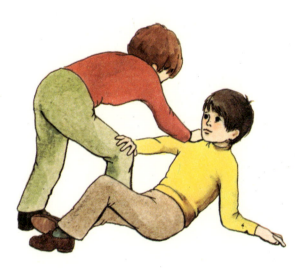

forward

To go forward is to go to a place in front.

fox

A fox is an animal It has a bushy tail.

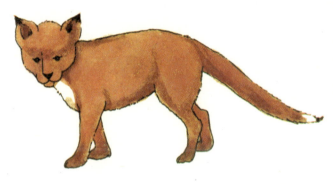

free

The bird is not caged. It is free. Anything you do not pay for is free.

Aa
Bb
Cc
Dd
Ee
Ff
Gg
Hh
Ii
Jj
Kk
Ll
Mm
Nn
Oo
Pp
Qq
Rr
Ss
Tt
Uu
Vv
Ww
Xx
Yy
Zz

Aa
Bb
Cc
Dd
Ee
Ff
Gg
Hh
Ii
Jj
Kk
Ll
Mm
Nn
Oo
Pp
Qq
Rr
Ss
Tt
Uu
Vv
Ww
Xx
Yy
Zz

freeze
To freeze something
is to turn it to ice.

fresh
The fruit is fresh.
It is not old.

Friday
Friday is the sixth day
of the week.

friend
A friend is someone you like.
Peter is Simon's friend.
They are happy together.

fright
Ann got a fright
when the balloon burst.
She was suddenly afraid.

frog
A frog is an animal
that lives near water.

fruit
Fruit grows on a
plant or a tree.
Some fruit is good to eat.

full
The box is full.
There is no more room in it.

fur
Fur is hair.
Many animals have fur
on their bodies.
It keeps them warm.

Gg

gale
A gale is a very strong wind.

gallop
When a horse gallops
it goes very fast.
Susan's pony likes to gallop.

game
We play a game for fun.
Simon and Tim are
having a game of marbles.

gap
A gap is an empty space
in the middle of something.
There is a gap in the fence.

garage
John's father keeps
his car in a garage.

garden
Mary plants seeds
in her garden.

Aa
Bb
Cc
Dd
Ee
Ff
Gg
Hh
Ii
Jj
Kk
Ll
Mm
Nn
Oo
Pp
Qq
Rr
Ss
Tt
Uu
Vv
Ww
Xx
Yy
Zz

Aa
Bb
Cc
Dd
Ee
Ff
Gg
Hh
Ii
Jj
Kk
Ll
Mm
Nn
Oo
Pp
Qq
Rr
Ss
Tt
Uu
Vv
Ww
Xx
Yy
Zz

gas
Gas feels like air.
We can cook with gas.

gentle
Ann's dog is gentle.
It is not rough and noisy.

geography
If you want to know about all
the lands in the world,
you should learn geography.

ghost
A ghost is supposed
to be the spirit of someone
who is dead.
Ghosts are not real.

giant
A giant is a very, very
large person.
We find giants only
in story books.

gift
Mark has given
his mother a gift.
He has given her a present.

glass
We can drink from a glass.
A window pane is made of glass.

goat
A goat is an animal.

good

Anything good is
not bad or nasty.
A good person is kind
and honest.

goose

A goose is a large white bird.
It makes a hissing
or cackling noise.

grain

Wheat and oats are grain.

grandfather

Your grandfather is the father
of your mother or your father.

grandmother

Your grandmother is the mother
of your mother or your father.

grape

A grape is a fruit.
Wine is made from grapes.

grapefruit

A grapefruit is a large
yellow fruit.
Do you ever eat grapefruit
for breakfast?

grass

Grass grows in the earth.

greedy

Someone who is greedy
wants more than his share.
This greedy boy wants
to eat all the buns.

green

Green is a colour.
Grass and leaves are green

Aa
Bb
Cc
Dd
Ee
Ff
Gg
Hh
Ii
Jj
Kk
Ll
Mm
Nn
Oo
Pp
Qq
Rr
Ss
Tt
Uu
Vv
Ww
Xx
Yy
Zz

Aa
Bb
Cc
Dd
Ee
Ff
Gg
Hh
Ii
Jj
Kk
Ll
Mm
Nn
Oo
Pp
Qq
Rr
Ss
Tt
Uu
Vv
Ww
Xx
Yy
Zz

grey
Grey is a colour.
The clouds are grey.

grip
To grip something is
to hold it firmly.
Tim has a good grip
on his hammer.

ground
The ground is the earth.
We walk on the ground.

grow
To grow is to get bigger.
The little bear will grow
as big as its mother.

grumble
Your mother will grumble
if you leave dirty footprints.
She will complain.

guard
To guard something
is to protect it.
A soldier who protects
an important building
is called a guard.

guess
If you don't know the answer,
have a guess.
You may guess correctly.

gun
A gun shoots out bullets.

guy
A guy is a dummy
made to look like a person.
Guy Fawkes tried to burn down
the Houses of Parliament.
On the fifth of November we
remember him, and that is why
we burn a guy.

Hh

habit
Simon has a habit
of swinging on the gate.
He does it often.

hail
Hail is rain that has
turned to ice.
It is cold and hard.

hair
We grow hair on our heads.
Men grow hair on their faces.

half
Cut the orange into
two equal parts.
Each part is one half
of the orange.

hamster
A hamster is a small animal

hand
You have four fingers and a
thumb on each hand.

harbour
A harbour is a shelter for ships.

hard
Hard means solid and not soft.
Hard also means not easy.

harm
To harm is to hurt.

Aa
Bb
Cc
Dd
Ee
Ff
Gg
Hh
Ii
Jj
Kk
Ll
Mm
Nn
Oo
Pp
Qq
Rr
Ss
Tt
Uu
Vv
Ww
Xx
Yy
Zz

harvest
Harvest is the time when the crops are ready for gathering on the farm.

hat
You wear a hat on your head.

hate
If you hate someone, you do not like that person at all.

hay
Hay is dried grass.
The farmer builds it into haystacks.

head
Your head is the top part of you.

health
When you are in good health, you are well.

heavy
Anything that is heavy is hard to lift.

hedgehog
A hedgehog is a small prickly animal.

helicopter
A helicopter flies in the air.

helmet
A policeman wears a helmet.
It is a hat to protect the head.

hide

Susan will hide behind
the rock.
No one will find her there.

high

When something is high
it is above most other things.
A mountain is high.

hill

A hill is a high
piece of ground.
A hill is not as high
as a mountain.

history

We learn history to find out
what happened long ago.

hive

A hive is a house for bees.

hole

A hole is an empty space.

holiday

When we are on holiday
we do something different.

hollow

Anything that is hollow
has a hole in it.

holly

A holly is a tree.
It has prickly leaves
and red berries.

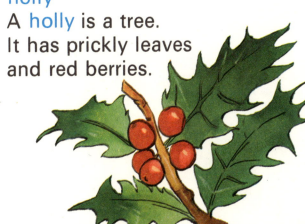

Aa
Bb
Cc
Dd
Ee
Ff
Gg
Hh
Ii
Jj
Kk
Ll
Mm
Nn
Oo
Pp
Qq
Rr
Ss
Tt
Uu
Vv
Ww
Xx
Yy
Zz

Aa
Bb
Cc
Dd
Ee
Ff
Gg
Hh
Ii
Jj
Kk
Ll
Mm
Nn
Oo
Pp
Qq
Rr
Ss
Tt
Uu
Vv
Ww
Xx
Yy
Zz

honey
Bees make honey
They put it in a honeycomb.

hood
A hood is a piece of cloth
that covers your head.

hook
You hang things up on a hook.
The cups are hanging on hooks.

horse
A horse is a useful animal.
We can ride on a horse.
Some horses pull things for us.

hospital
A hospital is a big building.
We go there when we are ill.
The doctors and nurses
at the hospital help us
to get well again.

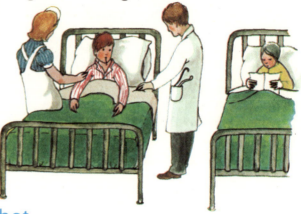

hot
Hot means very warm.

hour
An hour is a length of time.
There are sixty minutes
in an hour.

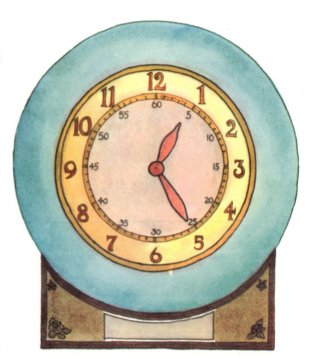

house
A house is a building
for people to live in.

hovercraft

A hovercraft moves along
just above the water
or the ground.
We can cross parts of
the sea in a hovercraft.

human

People are human.
Animals are not human.

hungry

If you are hungry,
you want food.

hunt

To hunt something is to look
for it, or to chase after it.
Tim has lost his pen.
He must hunt for it.

hurt

Susan has hurt her arm.
Her arm is sore.

hutch

A hutch is a house
for a small pet.
A rabbit lives in a hutch.

Aa
Bb
Cc
Dd
Ee
Ff
Gg
Hh
Ii
Jj
Kk
Ll
Mm
Nn
Oo
Pp
Qq
Rr
Ss
Tt
Uu
Vv
Ww
Xx
Yy
Zz

53

Aa
Bb
Cc
Dd
Ee
Ff
Gg
Hh
Ii
Jj
Kk
Ll
Mm
Nn
Oo
Pp
Qq
Rr
Ss
Tt
Uu
Vv
Ww
Xx
Yy
Zz

Ii

ice
Ice is frozen water.
In winter water often
turns to ice.

iceberg
An iceberg is a very large
lump of ice that floats
in the sea.

ice-cream
Ice-cream is cold and sweet.

ill
When we are ill,
we do not feel well.

important
Something that is important
is very special.
A king is an important person.

indoors
It is too wet to go out
and play.
The children will stay indoors.

infant
An infant is someone
very young.

ink

When you write with a pen
it must have ink in it.
If the pen has no ink
it will not mark the paper.

insect

An insect has six legs.
It usually has wings as well.

inside

The rubbish is in the dustbin.
It is inside the dustbin.

invite

John will invite Simon to tea.
He will ask him to come to tea.

iron

Mother will iron the clothes.
She will press them smooth
and flat with an iron.

island

An island is land
with water all around it.
It is not joined
to any other land.

ivy

Ivy is a climbing plant.
It climbs up walls.

Aa
Bb
Cc
Dd
Ee
Ff
Gg
Hh
Ii
Jj
Kk
Ll
Mm
Nn
Oo
Pp
Qq
Rr
Ss
Tt
Uu
Vv
Ww
Xx
Yy
Zz

Aa
Bb
Cc
Dd
Ee
Ff
Gg
Hh
Ii
Jj
Kk
Ll
Mm
Nn
Oo
Pp
Qq
Rr
Ss
Tt
Uu
Vv
Ww
Xx
Yy
Zz

Jj

jam
Jam is made with fruit.
It is sweet and sticky.

jar
We keep jam in a glass jar.

January
January is the first month
of the year.

jelly
Jelly is cold and wobbly.
Fruit jelly is good to eat.

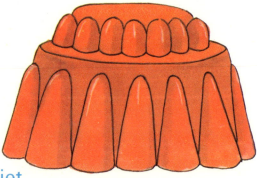

jet
A jet is a stream
of liquid or air.
A jet aeroplane shoots out jets
of air that drive it forward.

jewel
A jewel is a precious stone.

jigsaw
A jigsaw is a picture that is
cut up into little bits.

job
The baker is baking bread.
That is his job.

joint
A joint is a place where two
things join.

journey

Peter is going
on a long journey.
He has a long way to go.

jug

The lemonade is in the jug.

juice

The liquid part of anything
is its juice.
Do you like lemon juice?

July

July is the seventh month
of the year.
It is in the summertime.

jump

To jump is to leap in the air.
In the nursery rhyme,
the cow jumped over the moon.

June

June is the sixth month
of the year.
It is in the summertime.

jungle

A jungle is full of wild
tangled plants.
In hot countries
there are big jungles.

junk

Junk is rubbish.

Aa
Bb
Cc
Dd
Ee
Ff
Gg
Hh
Ii
Jj
Kk
Ll
Mm
Nn
Oo
Pp
Qq
Rr
Ss
Tt
Uu
Vv
Ww
Xx
Yy
Zz

Aa
Bb
Cc
Dd
Ee
Ff
Gg
Hh
Ii
Jj
Kk
Ll
Mm
Nn
Oo
Pp
Qq
Rr
Ss
Tt
Uu
Vv
Ww
Xx
Yy
Zz

kangaroo
A kangaroo is an animal
that lives in Australia.
A mother kangaroo carries her
baby in a kind of pocket
called a pouch.

keen
Keen means sharp.
A knife has a keen edge.
If you are keen about
something, you care about it.

keep
Jill will keep her old doll.
She will not throw it away.

kennel
A kennel is a house for a dog.

kettle
We boil water in a kettle.

kerb
The kerb is the edge
of the pavement.

key
A key is made of metal.
It is used to open
or shut a lock.
A piano has a different
kind of key.
We strike that to make
a musical sound.

kick

To kick something is
to hit it with your foot.

kind

When you are kind
you are good to other people.
It is kind of Tim to help
carry the shopping.
A kind of thing
is a sort of thing.
What kind of animal
do you like best?

kitchen

In the kitchen we make
food ready for eating.

kite

Mark is flying his kite.
Another kind of kite is a bird.

kitten

A kitten is a young cat.
A kitten loves to play
with wool or string.

knee

Your knee is the middle
joint of your leg.

knife

We use a knife to cut things.

Aa
Bb
Cc
Dd
Ee
Ff
Gg
Hh
Ii
Jj
Kk
Ll
Mm
Nn
Oo
Pp
Qq
Rr
Ss
Tt
Uu
Vv
Ww
Xx
Yy
Zz

Aa
Bb
Cc
Dd
Ee
Ff
Gg
Hh
Ii
Jj
Kk
Ll
Mm
Nn
Oo
Pp
Qq
Rr
Ss
Tt
Uu
Vv
Ww
Xx
Yy
Zz

knit
To knit is to make things
with loops of wool.
Mother will knit
a sweater for Peter.

knock
To knock is to hit
or rap something sharply.
Ann knocks at the door.

knot
There is a knot in the rope.
Two parts of the rope have
been tied together.

know
When you know something
you have learned about it.
Jill knows Mary.
She has learned a lot about her.

knuckle
A knuckle is the bone
at a finger joint.

koala
A koala is an animal
that lives in Australia.

Ll

lace
A lace is used for tying things together.
Can you tie your shoelaces?
Another kind of lace is cloth with a pattern of holes.

ladder
A ladder is something we climb to reach a higher place.

ladybird
A ladybird is a small spotted insect.

lake
A piece of water with land all around it is called a lake.

lamb
A lamb is a baby sheep.

lame
Someone who is lame cannot walk well.

lamp
A lamp is a small light.
Do you have a lamp beside your bed?

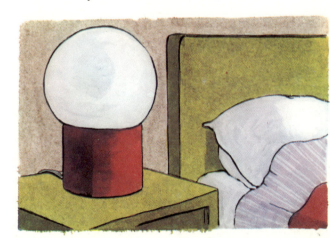

Aa
Bb
Cc
Dd
Ee
Ff
Gg
Hh
Ii
Jj
Kk
Ll
Mm
Nn
Oo
Pp
Qq
Rr
Ss
Tt
Uu
Vv
Ww
Xx
Yy
Zz

Aa
Bb
Cc
Dd
Ee
Ff
Gg
Hh
Ii
Jj
Kk
Ll
Mm
Nn
Oo
Pp
Qq
Rr
Ss
Tt
Uu
Vv
Ww
Xx
Yy
Zz

land
The solid parts of
the earth are land.

large
Something that is large
is very big.
Some buildings are large.

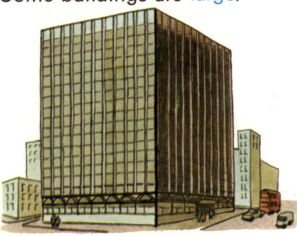

last
Last means after all others.
This is the last apple.
All the others have been eaten.

lawn
A lawn is grass that is
kept short and even.

lay
How many eggs did
the bird lay in its nest?

lazy
The tramp is lazy.
He does not want to work.

leaf
A leaf is part of a plant.

learn
You can learn how to
ride a bicycle.
You can find out how to do it.

least
Least means smallest
in size or in number.
Which jar has least sweets?

leather
Leather is the skin
of an animal.
This sandal is made of leather.

leave

To leave a place is to
go away from it.
To leave something also
means to let it stay.
If you do not finish
your dinner, you leave
some on your plate.

left

Have you left some
of your dinner?
Left also means
the opposite to right.
Do you know which
is your left hand?

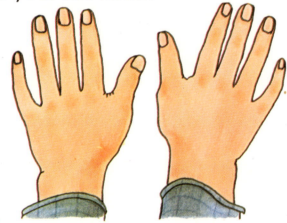

leg

You have a left leg and a
right leg.
Your legs help you to walk.

lemon

A lemon is a yellow fruit.

lend

Simon will lend his
knife to Tim.
He will let him keep it
for a short time.

less

Less means fewer,
or not as much as.
The pink flower has less
petals than the blue one.

lesson

A lesson is something
that is taught to us.

letter

Each letter of the alphabet
has a sound.
When you write a message to
someone, that is a letter.

lettuce

A lettuce is a vegetable.

Aa
Bb
Cc
Dd
Ee
Ff
Gg
Hh
Ii
Jj
Kk
Ll
Mm
Nn
Oo
Pp
Qq
Rr
Ss
Tt
Uu
Vv
Ww
Xx
Yy
Zz

Aa
Bb
Cc
Dd
Ee
Ff
Gg
Hh
Ii
Jj
Kk
Ll
Mm
Nn
Oo
Pp
Qq
Rr
Ss
Tt
Uu
Vv
Ww
Xx
Yy
Zz

level
Level means flat and even.
A table-top is level.

library
We keep books in a library.

lid
A lid is the top of something.
You can lift up a lid
or take it off.

lie
If you lie, you do not
tell the truth.
When you stretch out flat,
you also lie.

lift
When you lift something
you pick it up.

light
Out of doors the sun
gives us light.
Light also means not heavy.

lighthouse
A lighthouse shines
a bright light.
It tells ships at sea that
they are close to the land.

like

To like means to be fond of.
Mary likes her kitten.
Like also means similar.
Twins look like each other.

lion

A lion is a big, fierce animal.

liquid

You can pour a liquid.
Water and oil are liquids.

listen

Listen to the music.
Hear it and pay
attention to it.

little

Little means small
in size or in amount.
A mouse is little.
There is little juice
in the glass.

long

When something is long,
it goes on for some time
or for some distance.
When you long for something,
you wish for it.

look

Look at the picture.
See it and pay attention to it.

loose

Loose means free.
Something that is not caged
or tied up tightly is loose.
The leopard is loose.
It got out of its cage.

Aa
Bb
Cc
Dd
Ee
Ff
Gg
Hh
Ii
Jj
Kk
Ll
Mm
Nn
Oo
Pp
Qq
Rr
Ss
Tt
Uu
Vv
Ww
Xx
Yy
Zz

Aa
Bb
Cc
Dd
Ee
Ff
Gg
Hh
Ii
Jj
Kk
Ll
Mm
Nn
Oo
Pp
Qq
Rr
Ss
Tt
Uu
Vv
Ww
Xx
Yy
Zz

lorry
A lorry is a kind of wagon
with an engine.

lose
When you lose something
you cannot find it.

lot
A lot is much or many.
There are a lot
of grapes in this bunch.

loud
Loud means noisy.
The noise of the
aeroplane is loud.

love
To love means to like
very much.

low
Something that is low
is farther down
than other things.
This bird is flying low.

luck
When something happens
that you do not expect,
that is luck.
Tim found a penny.
he had good luck.
He was lucky.

Mm

machine

A machine has
parts that move.
It helps us to do things
more easily.
A washing machine helps
us to wash things quickly.

magnet

A magnet is a piece of iron.
It will pull anything else
made of iron towards it.

mail

All the letters and parcels
we post are mail.
The postman delivers the mail.

many

The squirrel has gathered
many nuts.
He has gathered a large
number of nuts.

map

A map is a drawing of a place.
It shows us where things
are in that place.
If you go to a strange place
you should take a map so that
you do not lose your way.

Aa
Bb
Cc
Dd
Ee
Ff
Gg
Hh
Ii
Jj
Kk
Ll
Mm
Nn
Oo
Pp
Qq
Rr
Ss
Tt
Uu
Vv
Ww
Xx
Yy
Zz

Aa
Bb
Cc
Dd
Ee
Ff
Gg
Hh
Ii
Jj
Kk
Ll
Mm
Nn
Oo
Pp
Qq
Rr
Ss
Tt
Uu
Vv
Ww
Xx
Yy
Zz

marble
Marble is a special
kind of stone.
A marble is a small round
glass ball.

March
March is the third month
of the year.

march
To march is to walk
quickly and steadily.

mark
You mark paper with a pencil.
The teacher gives you a good
mark if you have done well.

market
A market is a place where
things are bought and sold.

match
You strike a match
to get a flame.
Another kind of match
is a game.
When things match they are
like each other.

May
May is the fifth month
of the year.

maybe
Maybe the bus will come soon.
Perhaps it will come soon.

mean

What are you trying to say?
Explain what you mean.
Someone who is mean
likes to keep everything
for himself.

measles

Simon has measles.
He is covered with pink spots.
He does not feel well.

measure

When you measure, you judge
size or weight or distance.
Scales measure weight.

medicine

Medicine is something you
take when you are ill.
It helps you to get well.

melt

Heat can melt solid things.
It can turn them into liquid.
The sun's heat will
melt the snow.

mend

Father will mend
the broken chair.
He will make it whole again.

menu

A menu is a list that tells
you all the things
you may have to eat.

message

A message is what
you tell someone.
A letter is a message.
So is a telephone call.

Aa
Bb
Cc
Dd
Ee
Ff
Gg
Hh
Ii
Jj
Kk
Ll
Mm
Nn
Oo
Pp
Qq
Rr
Ss
Tt
Uu
Vv
Ww
Xx
Yy
Zz

Aa
Bb
Cc
Dd
Ee
Ff
Gg
Hh
Ii
Jj
Kk
Ll
Mm
Nn
Oo
Pp
Qq
Rr
Ss
Tt
Uu
Vv
Ww
Xx
Yy
Zz

middle

The middle is the centre.
The hole is in the middle
of the disc.

midnight

Midnight is twelve o'clock
at night.
It is the middle of the night.

milk

Milk is good for us.
All mothers give milk
to their babies.

minute

A minute is a short time.
There are sixty seconds
in a minute.

mirror

A mirror shows you a picture
of whatever is in front of it.

miss

To miss something is to fail
to hit it or to catch it.
You miss someone who
has gone away.

mistake

If you make a mistake
in your work, there will
be something wrong with it.

mix

Mother will mix the
flour and the sugar.

model

This is a model car.
It looks like a real car.

Monday

Monday is the second
day of the week.

money

We need money to pay
for what we buy.

monkey

A monkey is an animal.
Most monkeys are good
at climbing trees.

month

A month is four weeks.
There are twelve months
in every year.

moon

At night we may see the moon
in the sky.
It gives a white light.

mop

Mother uses a mop
to clean the floor.

more

There is more soup in the pot
than in the plate.
When you have finished,
would you like some more?

Aa
Bb
Cc
Dd
Ee
Ff
Gg
Hh
Ii
Jj
Kk
Ll
Mm
Nn
Oo
Pp
Qq
Rr
Ss
Tt
Uu
Vv
Ww
Xx
Yy
Zz

Aa
Bb
Cc
Dd
Ee
Ff
Gg
Hh
Ii
Jj
Kk
Ll
Mm
Nn
Oo
Pp
Qq
Rr
Ss
Tt
Uu
Vv
Ww
Xx
Yy
Zz

most
John has some money, Simon has more, but Peter has most. He has the largest amount.

moth
A moth is an insect

mountain
A very high hill is called a mountain.

motorway
A motorway is a big road with room for lots of cars and lorries.

mouse
A mouse is a small furry animal with a long tail.

mow

Father will mow the lawn.
He will cut the grass.

much

Do you have much to do?
Do you have a lot to do?

mud

Water and earth make mud.
Look at Ann.
She has been playing
in the mud.

muddle

Simon's toys are in a muddle.
They are all messed up.

mumps

When you have mumps
your face and neck swell up.

music

Sounds that are good to
listen to are called music.
John plays music
on his recorder.

must

Mary must hurry home before
she gets wet.
She has got to hurry home.

mystery

A mystery is something
we cannot explain.
How many stars are in the sky?
No one knows.
It is a mystery.

Aa
Bb
Cc
Dd
Ee
Ff
Gg
Hh
Ii
Jj
Kk
Ll
Mm
Nn
Oo
Pp
Qq
Rr
Ss
Tt
Uu
Vv
Ww
Xx
Yy
Zz

Aa
Bb
Cc
Dd
Ee
Ff
Gg
Hh
Ii
Jj
Kk
Ll
Mm
Nn
Oo
Pp
Qq
Rr
Ss
Tt
Uu
Vv
Ww
Xx
Yy
Zz

Nn

nail

A nail is the hard bit on a finger or toe.
A nail is also a piece of metal we use to fix two things together.

name

What is your name?
What are you called?
Can you name these things?

narrow

The street is narrow.
It is not broad.

navy

A navy is a lot of ships and the men who sail in them.
Navy is also a colour.
This hat is navy.

near

The tree is near the house.
It is not far from the house.

neat

The things on the shelf are neat.
They are not messy.
They are tidy.

neck
Your neck joins your head to your shoulders.

need
When you have a cold you need a handkerchief.

needle
A needle has a sharp point.
A sewing needle has an eye to put the thread through.

neighbour
Your neighbour is someone who is close to you.
Peter lives in the house next to Susan's.
He is her neighbour.

neither
Neither means not one nor another.
Which button is blue?
Neither button is blue.

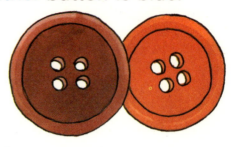

nest
A bird makes a cosy nest for its babies.
The nest is a shelter for them.

nettle
A nettle is a plant.
A stinging nettle has hairs on it that can hurt you.

never
Never means not at any time.

Aa
Bb
Cc
Dd
Ee
Ff
Gg
Hh
Ii
Jj
Kk
Ll
Mm
Nn
Oo
Pp
Qq
Rr
Ss
Tt
Uu
Vv
Ww
Xx
Yy
Zz

Aa
Bb
Cc
Dd
Ee
Ff
Gg
Hh
Ii
Jj
Kk
Ll
Mm
Nn
Oo
Pp
Qq
Rr
Ss
Tt
Uu
Vv
Ww
Xx
Yy
Zz

new

When something is new
it is not old.
New clothes are clothes that
have not been used before.

newspaper

Things that have just newly
happened are called news.
We read about the news
in a newspaper.

next

The pink house is next
to the blue house.
It is nearest to it.
Next year is the year that
comes after this year.

night

The moon comes out at night.
Night is the dark time
between one day and the next.

noise

A noise is a sound.

none

None means not any.
The sweets are finished.
There are none left.

ASSORTED MIX

nonsense

Nonsense is something silly.
This sum is nonsense.
It does not make sense.

1+2+3 = 46

noon

Noon is twelve o'clock in the morning. It is the middle of the day.

nose

Your nose is part of your face. You breathe through your nose.

nothing

There is nothing in the jug. There is not anything in it. It is empty. Nothing is also a number. It looks like 0.

November

November is the eleventh month of the year.

now

Do it now. Do it at this moment.

number

A number tells you how many there are. The number of kittens in the basket is five. 1, 2, 3, 4, 5, 6 are numbers.

nurse

A nurse looks after people who are ill or hurt.

nut

A nut is a hard fruit or seed. There is also a kind of nut that is a small piece of metal for a bolt to screw into.

Aa
Bb
Cc
Dd
Ee
Ff
Gg
Hh
Ii
Jj
Kk
Ll
Mm
Nn
Oo
Pp
Qq
Rr
Ss
Tt
Uu
Vv
Ww
Xx
Yy
Zz

Aa
Bb
Cc
Dd
Ee
Ff
Gg
Hh
Ii
Jj
Kk
Ll
Mm
Nn
Oo
Pp
Qq
Rr
Ss
Tt
Uu
Vv
Ww
Xx
Yy
Zz

Oo

oak
An oak is a tree
with very hard wood.
The fruit of the oak
is the acorn.

oar
An oar is a piece of wood that
is used to push a boat
through the water.

oats
Oats are grain.
The farmer grows oats
in his fields.
We use oats to make porridge.

obey
When we obey,
we do as we are told.
Tell the dog to fetch the ball.
He will obey you.

October
October is the tenth month
of the year.

odd
Odd means queer.
It also means not even.

often
We often go shopping.
We go shopping again and again.

oil

Oil is a greasy liquid.
We use oil for cooking.
A different kind of oil is used
to keep machines
running smoothly.

old

Old means not new.
This is a model
of an old ship.
People who are old
have lived for a long time.

once

Once means one time.
You can strike each match once.
You can strike it one time.

onion

An onion is a vegetable.
If you cut an onion it will
make your eyes sting.

open

The gate is open.
It is not shut.

opposite

The person opposite
you is the person directly
across from you.
Opposite also means
completely different.
Night is the opposite of day.

orange

An orange is a juicy fruit.

Aa
Bb
Cc
Dd
Ee
Ff
Gg
Hh
Ii
Jj
Kk
Ll
Mm
Nn
Oo
Pp
Qq
Rr
Ss
Tt
Uu
Vv
Ww
Xx
Yy
Zz

Aa
Bb
Cc
Dd
Ee
Ff
Gg
Hh
Ii
Jj
Kk
Ll
Mm
Nn
Oo
Pp
Qq
Rr
Ss
Tt
Uu
Vv
Ww
Xx
Yy
Zz

orchard
An orchard is a place where
lots of fruit trees grow.

oval
An oval is a curved shape.
An egg is oval.

oven
We cook in an oven.
We make the oven
as hot as we need it.

overalls
We wear overalls to protect
our clothes.
The workman wears
blue overalls.

owl
An owl is a bird that comes
out at night.
It has big eyes to help it to
see in the dark.

own
If you own something,
it belongs to you.
Peter owns a guinea pig.
It is his own guinea pig.

Pp

pain
When we are hurt we feel pain.
Simon has a sore leg.
He has a pain in his leg.

paint
The painter is painting
the wall.
He covers it with paint.

pair
Two things of the same kind
are a pair.
You have a pair of shoes
and a pair of gloves.

panda
A panda is a
black and white animal.

pane
A pane is a sheet of glass
in a window.
Some windows have many panes.

pantomime
A comic story acted in a
theatre is called a pantomime.
We go to the pantomime
at Christmas time.

Aa
Bb
Cc
Dd
Ee
Ff
Gg
Hh
Ii
Jj
Kk
Ll
Mm
Nn
Oo
Pp
Qq
Rr
Ss
Tt
Uu
Vv
Ww
Xx
Yy
Zz

D.—F

Aa
Bb
Cc
Dd
Ee
Ff
Gg
Hh
Ii
Jj
Kk
Ll
Mm
Nn
Oo
Pp
Qq
Rr
Ss
Tt
Uu
Vv
Ww
Xx
Yy
Zz

paper
This book is printed on paper.
We can write or paint
or draw on paper.

parcel
A parcel is something
wrapped up in paper.

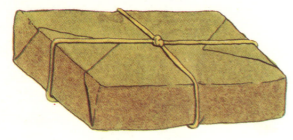

parent
A father is a parent.
A mother is also a parent.

park
A park is a big garden
that everyone can walk in.
A car park is a place where
cars can be left.

parrot
A parrot is a big bird.
Some parrots can speak.

part
Play with your friends.
Take part in their game.
A part of anything means some
of it, but not all.
When you part from someone,
you go away from him.

pass
Did you pass the pillar-box?
Did you go by it?
Please pass the pepper.
Please hand it over.

pattern
Something that has a pattern
has pictures all over it.
A pattern for clothes shows
us how to make them.

pavement

A pavement is a stone path.
When you walk along the road
you should stay on
the pavement.

peach

A peach is a fruit.

peacock

A peacock is a bird
with beautiful tail feathers.

pear

A pear is a fruit.

peel

Did you peel the banana?
Did you take off its skin?

pen

When we want to write or draw
with ink, we use a pen.
A pen is also a place
for keeping animals.

pencil

If we want to make marks
that we can rub out,
we write or draw with a pencil.

Aa
Bb
Cc
Dd
Ee
Ff
Gg
Hh
Ii
Jj
Kk
Ll
Mm
Nn
Oo
Pp
Qq
Rr
Ss
Tt
Uu
Vv
Ww
Xx
Yy
Zz

Aa
Bb
Cc
Dd
Ee
Ff
Gg
Hh
Ii
Jj
Kk
Ll
Mm
Nn
Oo
Pp
Qq
Rr
Ss
Tt
Uu
Vv
Ww
Xx
Yy
Zz

people
Men, women and children
are people.
We are all people.

perhaps
Perhaps the sun will
shine soon.
Maybe it will shine soon.

person
A person is a human being.

pet
A pet is an animal
you keep at home.

petal
A petal is part of a flower.

petrol
We put petrol into
a car to make it go.

photograph
A photograph is a picture
made by a camera.

piano
We can play music on a piano.

picnic
A picnic is a meal
we eat out-of-doors.

84

picture

You can paint a picture.
A photograph is also a picture.

pie

A pie is fruit or meat
with pastry on top.

piece

A piece of something is a
part of it.

pig

A pig is a farm animal.

pigeon

A pigeon is a bird.

pillow

A pillow is soft and
comfortable.
You can rest your head on it.

pine

A pine is a tree that stays
green all the year round.

pink

Pink is a colour.
This rose is pink.

pirate

A pirate is a sailor
who lived long ago.
Pirates attacked ships
and stole their treasure.

Aa
Bb
Cc
Dd
Ee
Ff
Gg
Hh
Ii
Jj
Kk
Ll
Mm
Nn
Oo
Pp
Qq
Rr
Ss
Tt
Uu
Vv
Ww
Xx
Yy
Zz

plain
Plain means clear and simple.
A plain is a flat piece
of land.

plenty
There are plenty of biscuits.
There are more than enough.

plum
A plum is a fruit.

pocket
A pocket is like a small bag
in our clothes.
We keep useful things
in a pocket.

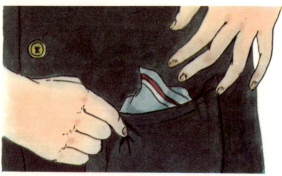

point
Point your finger at the door.
A point is a sharp end.

policeman
A policeman tries to keep
bad people from hurting other
people or stealing from them.

pony
A small horse is called a pony.

pool
A pool is a small lake.

potato
A potato is a vegetable.
Do you like mashed potatoes
or potato chips?

pram
Before a baby can walk,
he rides in a pram.

prepare
Father will prepare the tea.
He will get it ready.

present
The present time is now.
A present is a gift.

pretend
The children will pretend
to be cowboys.
They will make-believe
that they are cowboys.

price
What is the price
of the shirt?
How much does it cost?

prize
A prize is something nice.
If you do well at school,
you may win a prize.

Aa
Bb
Cc
Dd
Ee
Ff
Gg
Hh
Ii
Jj
Kk
Ll
Mm
Nn
Oo
Pp
Qq
Rr
Ss
Tt
Uu
Vv
Ww
Xx
Yy
Zz

Aa
Bb
Cc
Dd
Ee
Ff
Gg
Hh
Ii
Jj
Kk
Ll
Mm
Nn
Oo
Pp
Qq
Rr
Ss
Tt
Uu
Vv
Ww
Xx
Yy
Zz

promise
When we make a promise,
we say we will do something.

puddle
A puddle is a small pool.

pupil
The black circle in your eye
is called the pupil.
A pupil is also someone
who is learning.

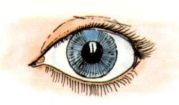

puppet
A puppet is a doll
that is moved by strings.

puppy
A puppy is a baby dog.

purple
Purple is a colour.
This flower is purple.

purse
We carry money in a
small bag called a purse.

pyjamas
We put on our pyjamas
to go to bed.

Qq

quarrel
When we quarrel
we say angry words.

quarter
Break the chocolate into
four equal parts.
Each part will be a
quarter of the chocolate.

queer
Queer means odd or strange.
Susan is wearing her
father's clothes.
She looks queer.

question
What is the time?
That is a question.
When you want to know
anything, ask a question.

quick
The mouse is too quick
for the cat.
It runs too fast for
the cat to catch it.

quiet
It is quiet in the country.
There are no loud noises.

quite
The cake is quite
ready for eating.
It is completely ready.

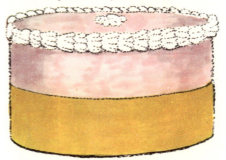

Aa
Bb
Cc
Dd
Ee
Ff
Gg
Hh
Ii
Jj
Kk
Ll
Mm
Nn
Oo
Pp
Qq
Rr
Ss
Tt
Uu
Vv
Ww
Xx
Yy
Zz

Aa
Bb
Cc
Dd
Ee
Ff
Gg
Hh
Ii
Jj
Kk
Ll
Mm
Nn
Oo
Pp
Qq
Rr
Ss
Tt
Uu
Vv
Ww
Xx
Yy
Zz

Rr

race
A race is held to see
who is fastest.
This is a horse race.
The fastest horse
will win the race.

radio
We can listen to music
on the radio.
The music is sent by
radio from another place.

rag
A rag is a piece of old cloth.

railway
Trains run along railway lines.

rainbow
A rainbow is a curved
band of colours in the sky.
We can see a rainbow
when the sun shines
through the rain.

raspberry
A raspberry is a soft fruit.

rat

A rat is a small animal.

raw

The celery is raw.
It has not been cooked.

reach

The shelf is too high for Ann.
She is not able to reach it.

read

To read is to look at and
understand.
Can you read this book?

real

The children have a
doll's house.
It is not a real house.
They live in a real house.

reason

We use our reason
when we think.
It helps us
to understand things.
The reason we wash things
is to make them clean.

receive

To receive is to get.
Did you receive many
birthday presents?

Aa
Bb
Cc
Dd
Ee
Ff
Gg
Hh
Ii
Jj
Kk
Ll
Mm
Nn
Oo
Pp
Qq
Rr
Ss
Tt
Uu
Vv
Ww
Xx
Yy
Zz

Aa
Bb
Cc
Dd
Ee
Ff
Gg
Hh
Ii
Jj
Kk
Ll
Mm
Nn
Oo
Pp
Qq
Rr
Ss
Tt
Uu
Vv
Ww
Xx
Yy
Zz

red
Red is a colour.
This car is red.

refuse
When you refuse to
do something,
you will not do it.

reindeer
A reindeer is an animal that
lives in cold countries.

remember
Try to remember what
you have learned.
Try not to forget it.

remove
To remove is to take away.
If you go to live in a new
house, a removal van will
remove your furniture from
your old house and take it
to your new house.

reply
A reply is an answer.

rescue
If you save someone from
danger, you rescue him.

rest
This girl is tired.
She will lie down and rest.
The rest of the children
will play.

return
When school is over, the
children return to their homes.

rhubarb
Rhubarb is a vegetable.
We eat rhubarb tart.

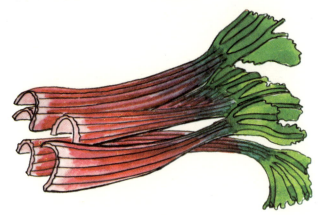

rice
Rice is white seeds.
This is a rice pudding.

rich
Rich means having a lot
of something.
Rich people have a lot of money.

right
Right is the opposite of left.
Do you write with
your right hand?
Right also means correct.
Do you know the right time?

ring
You can wear a ring
on your finger.
A ring is also the
sound a bell makes.

rise
Did you rise early
this morning?
Did you get up early?

river
A river is a long stream
of water.

Aa
Bb
Cc
Dd
Ee
Ff
Gg
Hh
Ii
Jj
Kk
Ll
Mm
Nn
Oo
Pp
Qq
Rr
Ss
Tt
Uu
Vv
Ww
Xx
Yy
Zz

Aa
Bb
Cc
Dd
Ee
Ff
Gg
Hh
Ii
Jj
Kk
Ll
Mm
Nn
Oo
Pp
Qq
Rr
Ss
Tt
Uu
Vv
Ww
Xx
Yy
Zz

road

A road is a way from
one place to another.
Cars drive along the road.
We must take care crossing
the road.

rob

To rob is to steal.
A robber steals things
that belong to other people.

robin

A robin is a bird
with a red breast.

rock

To rock something is to move it
backwards and forwards.
A rock is also a lump of stone.

rocket

A rocket shoots into the air.

roof

The barn has a red roof.
The house has a thatched roof.

room
The bus is full.
There is no more room in it.
A bedroom is a room.

root
The root of a plant
grows under the ground.

round
Round is a shape.
A roundabout goes
round and round.

row
A row is a line of things.
Here is a row of skittles.
To row a boat is to drive it
through the water with oars.

rub
Rub your hands together.
Move them up and down
against each other.

rubbish
Rubbish is anything
we no longer want.

rug
A rug is a warm cover.
You can put a rug on the floor.
You can put a rug
over your legs.

rush
To rush is to hurry.
A rush is a tall plant
that grows near water.

Aa
Bb
Cc
Dd
Ee
Ff
Gg
Hh
Ii
Jj
Kk
Ll
Mm
Nn
Oo
Pp
Qq
Rr
Ss
Tt
Uu
Vv
Ww
Xx
Yy
Zz

Aa
Bb
Cc
Dd
Ee
Ff
Gg
Hh
Ii
Jj
Kk
Ll
Mm
Nn
Oo
Pp
Qq
Rr
Ss
Tt
Uu
Vv
Ww
Xx
Yy
Zz

Ss

safe

When you are safe, you are not in any danger.

sail

A sail is a sheet of cloth that catches the wind and helps it blow a boat along.
To sail is to travel by water.
A sailor sails all over the world.

sale

The things in the shop are there for you to buy.
They are on sale.

salt

Salt is a white powder.
We put salt on our food to give it more taste.
The water in the sea is salt water.

sand

There is sand on the beach at the seaside.
Have you ever built a sandcastle?

sandwich

A sandwich is two slices of bread with some other kind of food between them.

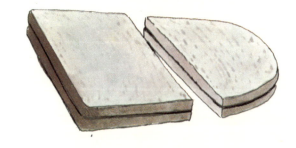

Saturday

Saturday is the seventh day of the week.

save

To save something
is to keep it safe.

scarecrow

The farmer puts a scarecrow
in his field.
It frightens away the birds
that want to eat the seeds.

school

We go to school
to learn lessons.

sea

A sea is a large stretch
of salt water.
Seaweed grows in the sea.
Sea gulls are birds
that live by the sea.

seal

A seal is a furry animal
that swims in the sea.
To seal something is to close
it by sticking it down.

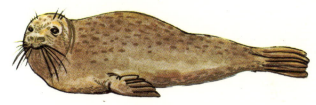

season

A season is a part
of the year.
Every year has four seasons —
spring, summer, autumn, winter.

Aa
Bb
Cc
Dd
Ee
Ff
Gg
Hh
Ii
Jj
Kk
Ll
Mm
Nn
Oo
Pp
Qq
Rr
Ss
Tt
Uu
Vv
Ww
Xx
Yy
Zz

Aa
Bb
Cc
Dd
Ee
Ff
Gg
Hh
Ii
Jj
Kk
Ll
Mm
Nn
Oo
Pp
Qq
Rr
Ss
Tt
Uu
Vv
Ww
Xx
Yy
Zz

second

A second is a small amount
of time.
There are sixty seconds
in a minute.
Second also means the one
after first.
The red bus is the second one.

seed

A seed is a thing from which
other things grow.
This thistle grew from a seed.

September
September is the ninth
month of the year.
It is in autumn.

shadow
When the sun is low,
you cast a long shadow.

share
Ann will share out her sweets.
Everyone will get
a share of them.

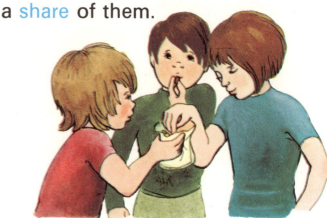

sharp
Anything that is sharp has
a point, or can cut.

sheep
A sheep is an animal
with a thick fleece.
We get wool from sheep.

shell
A shell is a cover.

shelter
A shelter keeps you safe
or warm or dry.

ship
A ship is a big boat.

shop
A shop is a place
where things are sold.
This is a fish shop.

short
Something that is short
is not long, or not tall.
A stocking is long.
A sock is short.

shoulder
Your shoulder is the part of
you where each arm joins on.

shut
The gate is shut.
It is closed.

side
The boy is fishing at the side
of the river.
He has a basket by his side.

silly
Silly means foolish.

simple
It is simple to add
two and two.
It is easy.

Aa
Bb
Cc
Dd
Ee
Ff
Gg
Hh
Ii
Jj
Kk
Ll
Mm
Nn
Oo
Pp
Qq
Rr
Ss
Tt
Uu
Vv
Ww
Xx
Yy
Zz

sink
If a boat has an accident,
it may sink.
It may fall down
through the water.
We wash the dishes in the sink.

sister
A girl is the sister of the
other children in the family.

skate
When the pond is frozen
the children skate on it.
They slide over the ice
on their skates.

skin
Skin is a covering.
The sun turns our skin brown.

sky
The sky is the open space
above us.

smack
To smack is to hit sharply.

small
Small means little.
A mole is a small animal.

smoke
Smoke is the clouds
that come from fire.

snail

A snail is a small creature that crawls along the ground. It has a shell on its back.

snake

A snake also crawls along the ground. Some snakes are dangerous.

sneeze

When your nose tickles, you sneeze.
If you have a cold, you sneeze a lot.

snow

Snow is soft and cold.
It falls down from the sky.
Have you ever built a snowman with the snow?

soap

We use soap for washing.

soft

Fur is soft.
It is not hard.

solid

Anything that is not a liquid or a gas is solid.

son

A boy is the son of his father and mother.

soon

The buds will soon open. In a short time they will open into leaves.

sorry

When we feel sorry we wish something had not happened.
Jill is sorry she broke the cup.

Aa
Bb
Cc
Dd
Ee
Ff
Gg
Hh
Ii
Jj
Kk
Ll
Mm
Nn
Oo
Pp
Qq
Rr
Ss
Tt
Uu
Vv
Ww
Xx
Yy
Zz

Aa
Bb
Cc
Dd
Ee
Ff
Gg
Hh
Ii
Jj
Kk
Ll
Mm
Nn
Oo
Pp
Qq
Rr
Ss
Tt
Uu
Vv
Ww
Xx
Yy
Zz

sour
A lemon is sour.
It is not sweet.

sparrow
A sparrow is a small
brown bird.

spider
A spider is an animal
with eight legs.
It spins a web to catch flies.

spill
Peter let the water spill.
He let it fall
out of the bucket.

spring
Spring is a season.
A spring is water that
comes out of the ground.
Another kind of spring
is a coil of wire.
A frog can spring
from one stone to another.

square
Square is a shape
with four equal sides.
The fountain is in
the town square.

squirrel
A squirrel is a small animal
with a bushy tail.
It lives in the trees.

stair

A stair is one of
a row of steps.
Do you have stairs
in your house?

stamp

Stamp your foot
on the ground.
Strike it hard on the ground.
Before you post a letter,
you should stick
a stamp on it.

star

A star is big, but it looks
tiny because it is
so far away.
It looks like a twinkling
light in the sky at night.

station

We go to a railway station
to get on to a train.
Buses are kept in
a bus station.

steam

Steam is the clouds
that come from hot liquid.

steep

The hill is steep.
It slopes sharply.

Aa
Bb
Cc
Dd
Ee
Ff
Gg
Hh
Ii
Jj
Kk
Ll
Mm
Nn
Oo
Pp
Qq
Rr
Ss
Tt
Uu
Vv
Ww
Xx
Yy
Zz

Aa
Bb
Cc
Dd
Ee
Ff
Gg
Hh
Ii
Jj
Kk
Ll
Mm
Nn
Oo
Pp
Qq
Rr
Ss
Tt
Uu
Vv
Ww
Xx
Yy
Zz

stick

A stick is a piece of wood.
Tim pushes his boat
with a stick.
To stick something
is to fix it firmly.

stiff

Anything that is stiff
will not bend easily.

stone

A stone is a piece of rock.

storm

A storm is very bad weather.

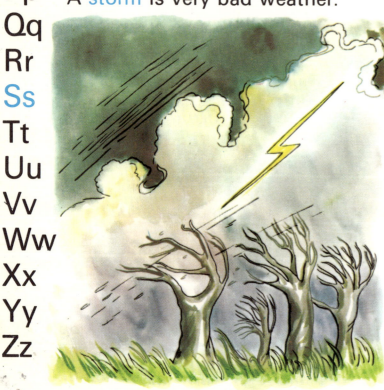

straight

Something that is straight
has no bends in it.

straw

Straw is dried and cut grain.
A straw is also a tube.

strawberry

A strawberry is a soft fruit.

strong

Strong means tough and solid.
A strong person is healthy.
Some foods have a strong taste.

suck

To suck something
is to draw it in.

summer

Summer is a season.
It is the warmest season
of the year.

sun

The sun shines in the sky.

Sunday
Sunday is the first
day of the week.
Most people have
a holiday on Sunday.

sure
When we know that something
is a fact, we are sure of it.

swallow
A swallow is a small bird
with a forked tail.
To swallow something
is to eat it up.

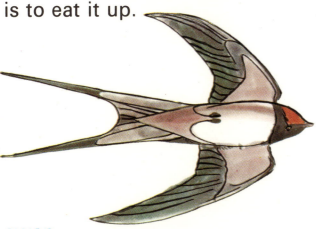

swan
A swan is a large white bird
that lives on the water.

sweep
We sweep up the crumbs
with a brush.
A sweep is a man who sweeps
the soot out of chimneys.

sweet
Sweet things are not sour.
Honey and jam are very sweet.

swim
When you swim you push
yourself through the water.
Have you learned how to swim?

swing
A swing is a seat hung
on ropes or chains.
It can swing backwards
and forwards.

Aa
Bb
Cc
Dd
Ee
Ff
Gg
Hh
Ii
Jj
Kk
Ll
Mm
Nn
Oo
Pp
Qq
Rr
Ss
Tt
Uu
Vv
Ww
Xx
Yy
Zz

Aa
Bb
Cc
Dd
Ee
Ff
Gg
Hh
Ii
Jj
Kk
Ll
Mm
Nn
Oo
Pp
Qq
Rr
Ss
Tt
Uu
Vv
Ww
Xx
Yy
Zz

Tt

tail
The tail of something is the part behind the other parts.
A dog can wag its tail.

tale
A tale is a story.
Do you like fairy tales?

tall
Anything that stretches a long way up is tall.
The church tower is tall.

tame
A tame animal is not wild.

taste
When we eat something we taste it.
Ice-cream has a sweet taste.
Lemon juice tastes sour.

tea
Tea is made from the dried leaves of the tea plant.
It is good to drink.

telephone
A telephone carries sound over a distance.
Have you spoken to a friend on the telephone?

television
Television is a way of sending pictures through space from one place to another.
We watch the pictures on a television set.

temper
When you are cross you are in a bad temper.
When you are happy you are in a good temper.

tent
A tent is a shelter that you can fold up and carry around.

third
Third is the one after second.
The cake is cut into three equal parts.
Each part is a third of the cake.

throw
Jill threw the ball to Peter.
She tossed it towards him.
It was a good throw.

thumb
You have one thumb on each hand.

Thursday
Thursday is the fifth day of the week.

tick
Listen to the clock tick.
This mark √ is also a tick.

Aa
Bb
Cc
Dd
Ee
Ff
Gg
Hh
Ii
Jj
Kk
Ll
Mm
Nn
Oo
Pp
Qq
Rr
Ss
Tt
Uu
Vv
Ww
Xx
Yy
Zz

Aa
Bb
Cc
Dd
Ee
Ff
Gg
Hh
Ii
Jj
Kk
Ll
Mm
Nn
Oo
Pp
Qq
Rr
Ss
Tt
Uu
Vv
Ww
Xx
Yy
Zz

ticket

When we ride in a bus
or train, we buy a ticket.
It is a small piece of paper
that shows we have paid
for our journey.

tie

Boys often wear a tie.
To tie something is to
fasten it with a knot.

tiger

A tiger is a fierce animal.
It is a very large kind of cat.

tin

We buy some foods in a tin.
The tin is made of a metal
called tin

tiny

This is a tiny insect.
It is very, very small.

tired

Father has been working hard.
Now he feels tired.
He needs to rest.

toast

Toast is bread heated
till it is crisp.
We toast the bread
in a toaster.

today

What have you done today?
What have you done
on this day?

toe

We have five toes on each foot.
Each toe has a nail.

tomato

A tomato is a fruit.

tomorrow

Tomorrow is the day
that is coming next.

too

Mark's jacket is too small
for him.
It is smaller than it should be.
His sweater is small, too.
It is also small.

tool

A tool is something we use
to help us in our work.
A spade is a gardening tool.
A hammer and a saw
are tools for woodwork.

top

On top means
at the highest part.
The baby has a spinning top.

torch

A torch is a light
you can carry.

Aa
Bb
Cc
Dd
Ee
Ff
Gg
Hh
Ii
Jj
Kk
Ll
Mm
Nn
Oo
Pp
Qq
Rr
Ss
Tt
Uu
Vv
Ww
Xx
Yy
Zz

Aa
Bb
Cc
Dd
Ee
Ff
Gg
Hh
Ii
Jj
Kk
Ll
Mm
Nn
Oo
Pp
Qq
Rr
Ss
Tt
Uu
Vv
Ww
Xx
Yy
Zz

tortoise

A tortoise is a small animal
with a hard shell on its back.

tough

Anything that is tough
does not break or tear easily.

towel

A towel is a soft cloth
for drying people or things.

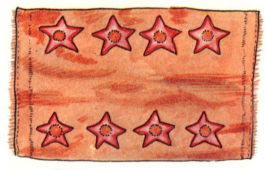

town

There are lots of houses and
shops in a town.
A town is not as big as a city.

toy

A toy is something
to play with.
Can you name these toys?

tractor

A farmer uses a tractor.
It pulls all the machines
he needs on the farm.

traffic

Traffic is everything that
moves on the road.
Cars, buses, lorries, bicycles
and people are traffic.

train
A train goes along
railway lines.
It takes people or things
from one place to another.

tree
A tree is a large plant.

trip
When we fall over
something, we trip.
A trip also means
an outing, or a journey.

true
Anything that is true
is a fact.

try
Try not to fall in the water.
Do your best not to fall.

tube
A tube is long and rounded.
It is hollow inside.

Tuesday
Tuesday is the third
day of the week.

tunnel
A tunnel is a passage
that goes under the ground.

turkey
A turkey is a big bird
that lives on a farm.

twice
Twice means two times.

tyre
A tyre is the band round
the outside of a wheel.
A tyre is usually
made of rubber.

Aa
Bb
Cc
Dd
Ee
Ff
Gg
Hh
Ii
Jj
Kk
Ll
Mm
Nn
Oo
Pp
Qq
Rr
Ss
Tt
Uu
Vv
Ww
Xx
Yy
Zz

Aa
Bb
Cc
Dd
Ee
Ff
Gg
Hh
Ii
Jj
Kk
Ll
Mm
Nn
Oo
Pp
Qq
Rr
Ss
Tt
Uu
Vv
Ww
Xx
Yy
Zz

Uu

ugly
Something that is ugly
is nasty to look at.

umbrella
John is holding an umbrella
above his head.
The umbrella shelters him
from the rain.

unable
Simon is unable to squeeze
through the gap in the fence.
He is not able
to get through.

uncle
Your uncle is your mother's
or your father's brother.

under
Ann is hiding under
the table.
She is hiding below
the table.

understand
To understand something
is to know what it means,
or how it works.

undo
Jane will undo the parcel.
She has loosened the string
and unstuck the paper.

undress

We undress when we go to bed.
We take our clothes off.

unhappy

When you are unhappy
you feel sad.

uniform

A uniform is a set
of special clothes.
A soldier wears a uniform.
So does a fireman.
Their uniform tells us
the kind of job they do.

unkind

To be unkind is to hurt
people or make them unhappy.

unless

Unless you turn off the tap,
the water will spill out.
If you do not turn it off,
the water will spill out.

until

Until it is three o'clock
the children must stay
in school.

Aa
Bb
Cc
Dd
Ee
Ff
Gg
Hh
Ii
Jj
Kk
Ll
Mm
Nn
Oo
Pp
Qq
Rr
Ss
Tt
Uu
Vv
Ww
Xx
Yy
Zz

.D.—H

Aa
Bb
Cc
Dd
Ee
Ff
Gg
Hh
Ii
Jj
Kk
Ll
Mm
Nn
Oo
Pp
Qq
Rr
Ss
Tt
Uu
Vv
Ww
Xx
Yy
Zz

unusual

It is unusual for the paper-boy to come on foot. He usually comes on his bicycle.

unwilling

If you are unwilling to do something, you do not want to do it.

upright

The trees are upright. They are standing straight up.

upset

Peter upset the paint pot. He knocked it over.

upside-down

Mary is standing on her head. She is upside-down.

upstairs

Susan is going up to her bedroom. She is going upstairs.

urgent

Anything that is urgent must be done at once.

use

We use a broom to sweep with. That is the use of a broom. It helps us because it is useful.

Vv

valley
A valley is a hollow in the land.

van
A van is a kind of car that carries things.
This is a mail van.
It carries parcels.

vase
We put flowers in a vase.
There is water in the vase.

vegetable
A vegetable is a plant that we can eat.
Can you name these vegetables?

vein
A vein is a kind of tube.
The veins in your body carry the blood all through it.

velvet
Velvet is a kind of cloth that feels very soft.

Aa
Bb
Cc
Dd
Ee
Ff
Gg
Hh
Ii
Jj
Kk
Ll
Mm
Nn
Oo
Pp
Qq
Rr
Ss
Tt
Uu
Vv
Ww
Xx
Yy
Zz

Aa
Bb
Cc
Dd
Ee
Ff
Gg
Hh
Ii
Jj
Kk
Ll
Mm
Nn
Oo
Pp
Qq
Rr
Ss
Tt
Uu
Vv
Ww
Xx
Yy
Zz

vet
A vet is a doctor for animals.

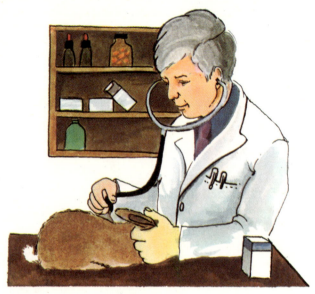

view
The view is what we can see.
Do you have a nice view
from your window?

village
A village has a few streets
and houses and shops.
A village is not as big
as a town.

violet
A violet is a spring flower.
Violet is also a colour.
It is the colour of a violet.

violin
We can play music on a violin.
It is made of wood
and it has four strings.

visit
Susan has come to see Jill.
She has come to visit her.
She is Jill's visitor.

voice
The sounds you make through
your mouth are your voice.
You can use your voice
to speak or to sing.

Ww

wade

Do you like to wade?
Do you like to walk
in the water?

wag

See the dog wag its tail.
It moves its tail from
side to side.

wage

A wage is the money we
are paid for the work we do.

wagon

A wagon is for moving
heavy loads.
Long ago people travelled
over long distances in
a covered wagon.

waist

Simon wears a belt
round his waist.

Aa
Bb
Cc
Dd
Ee
Ff
Gg
Hh
Ii
Jj
Kk
Ll
Mm
Nn
Oo
Pp
Qq
Rr
Ss
Tt
Uu
Vv
Ww
Xx
Yy
Zz

P.D.—H*

Aa
Bb
Cc
Dd
Ee
Ff
Gg
Hh
Ii
Jj
Kk
Ll
Mm
Nn
Oo
Pp
Qq
Rr
Ss
Tt
Uu
Vv
Ww
Xx
Yy
Zz

wait

The people must wait
to cross the river.
They must stay till
the ferryboat comes.

wake

When we wake up,
we stop sleeping.

walk

To walk is to travel on foot.
The children walk down the
lane to meet their friends.

wall

A wall is a strong fence made
of stone or brick.
Each side of a building is
a wall, and there are walls
inside it too.

war

A war is a big quarrel
amongst lots of people.
Soldiers fight many battles
in a war.

warm

In spring the days
are often warm.
They are not cold,
but they are not too hot.

wash

To wash is to clean with
soap and water.
This girl is washing her hair.

wasp

A wasp is a striped insect.
It has a nasty sting
in its tail.

waste

When we waste something we
do not make good use of it,
or we spoil it.
We throw waste paper
in a waste-basket.

watch

John will watch the race.
He will go on looking at it.
A watch is a clock.
Do you have a wrist-watch?

wave

When things wave, they
move in the air.
You wave your hand
when you say goodbye.
A wave in the sea is
moving water.

Aa
Bb
Cc
Dd
Ee
Ff
Gg
Hh
Ii
Jj
Kk
Ll
Mm
Nn
Oo
Pp
Qq
Rr
Ss
Tt
Uu
Vv
Ww
Xx
Yy
Zz

119

Aa
Bb
Cc
Dd
Ee
Ff
Gg
Hh
Ii
Jj
Kk
Ll
Mm
Nn
Oo
Pp
Qq
Rr
Ss
Tt
Uu
Vv
Ww
Xx
Yy
Zz

weak
Weak means not strong.

weather
In bad weather it rains or it
snows or cold winds blow.
In good weather the sun shines
and the wind is soft.
A weathervane tells us
which way the wind blows.

Wednesday
Wednesday is the fourth
day of the week.

week
A week has seven days —
Sunday, Monday, Tuesday,
Wednesday, Thursday, Friday
and Saturday.

weigh
We weigh things to find out
how heavy they are.

wellington
A wellington is a rubber boot
for wearing in wet weather.
Mary has red wellingtons.

whale
A whale is a large animal.
It looks like a fish
and it lives in the sea.
A whale is the biggest
creature in the sea.

wheel

A wheel can turn round
and round.
A car has wheels.

whisper

To whisper is to talk
very softly.

white

Something that is white
has no colour at all.
A snowdrop is a white flower.

whole

The orange is whole.
It is all there.
The apple is not whole.
A part of it is missing.

wide

The river is wide.
It is broad.
It is not narrow.

wild

A hippopotamus is
a wild animal.
It is not tame.

wind

Wind is air that moves.
When the wind blows hard,
the sails of the windmill
go round and round.

window

A window is an opening
that lets in light.
It is usually covered
with glass.

Aa
Bb
Cc
Dd
Ee
Ff
Gg
Hh
Ii
Jj
Kk
Ll
Mm
Nn
Oo
Pp
Qq
Rr
Ss
Tt
Uu
Vv
Ww
Xx
Yy
Zz

Aa
Bb
Cc
Dd
Ee
Ff
Gg
Hh
Ii
Jj
Kk
Ll
Mm
Nn
Oo
Pp
Qq
Rr
Ss
Tt
Uu
Vv
Ww
Xx
Yy
Zz

wing
A wing is used for flying.
Anything that flies has wings.

winter
Winter is a season
It is the coldest season
of the year.

witch
A witch is an old woman who
can do magic things.
A witch is not real.
We can read about witches
in story books.

wood
We get wood from trees.
This chest is made of wood
A wood is a group of trees.

wool
Wool is the soft hair
that grows on a sheep.

world
The world is the whole earth
and all the people
that live on it.

worm
A worm is a creature with
no legs and no backbone.

write
To write is to draw the shapes
of letters and words.

wrong
Wrong means not right.
The picture is
the wrong way up.

Xx

X-ray

An X-ray is a special kind of photograph.
A doctor uses an X-ray to take a picture of the inside of your body.

xylophone

We can play music on a xylophone.
It has a row of keys that we can strike with a little hammer.

Yy

yacht

A yacht is a small ship with sails.
Have you ever seen a yacht race?

yawn

We yawn when we feel tired.
We stretch our mouths wide open when we yawn.

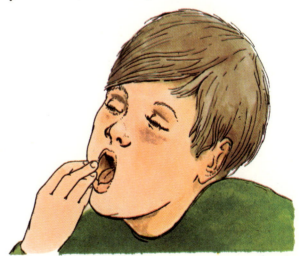

Aa
Bb
Cc
Dd
Ee
Ff
Gg
Hh
Ii
Jj
Kk
Ll
Mm
Nn
Oo
Pp
Qq
Rr
Ss
Tt
Uu
Vv
Ww
Xx
Yy
Zz

Aa
Bb
Cc
Dd
Ee
Ff
Gg
Hh
Ii
Jj
Kk
Ll
Mm
Nn
Oo
Pp
Qq
Rr
Ss
Tt
Uu
Vv
Ww
Xx
Yy
Zz

year
There are fifty-two weeks
in a year.
There are twelve months
in a year.
A year has four seasons.
A calendar lists all the days
and weeks and months in a year

yellow
Yellow is a colour.
Can you name all the yellow
things in this picture?

yesterday
Yesterday means the day
before today
If today is Friday, yesterday
must have been Thursday.

yolk
The yolk is the yellow
part of an egg.
It is round.

young
Young means not old.
The woman is young.
The baby is very young.
The man sitting on
the bench is not young.
He is old.

124

Zz

zebra

A zebra is a wild animal.
It looks like a horse
with stripes.

zoo

A zoo is a park where
wild animals are kept
in cages or pens.
Have you ever been to see
the animals in the zoo?

Aa
Bb
Cc
Dd
Ee
Ff
Gg
Hh
Ii
Jj
Kk
Ll
Mm
Nn
Oo
Pp
Qq
Rr
Ss
Tt
Uu
Vv
Ww
Xx
Yy
Zz

One 1 whale

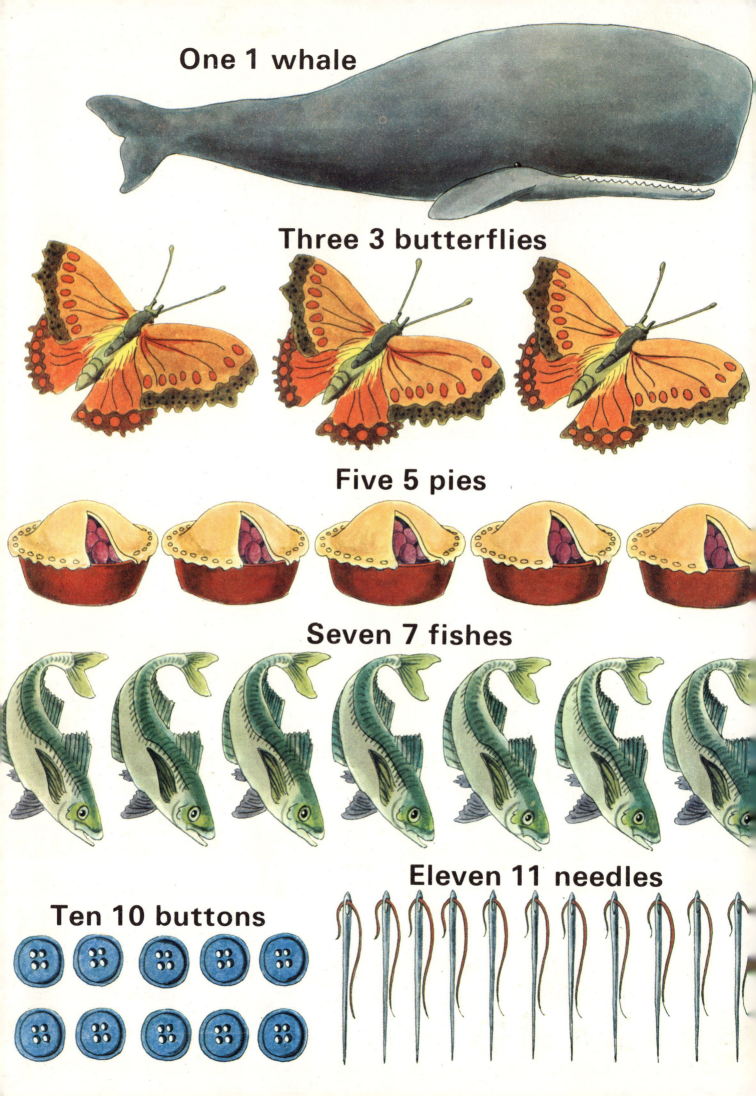

Three 3 butterflies

Five 5 pies

Seven 7 fishes

Eleven 11 needles

Ten 10 buttons